Ron Sukenick's Tips on Expanding your Business by Building Relationships

Dynamic Presenter, Best Selling Author, LinkedIn Expert and Intuitive Business Coach

Richard G Lowe, Jr

Ron Sukenick's Tips on Expanding your Business by Building Relationships

Dynamic Presenter, Best Selling Author, LinkedIn Expert and Intuitive Business Coach

Interviews with Influencers Series #2

Published by The Writing King
www.thewritingking.com

Ron Sukenick's Tips on Expanding your Business by Building Relationships

Copyright © 2016 by Richard G Lowe, Jr.

Cover Artist: theamateurzone

Library of Congress Control Number: 2016920138

ASIN: B01GY8J8YA
ISBN: 978-1-943517-34-3 (Paperback)
ISBN: 978-1-943517-33-6 (eBook)

.

Table of Contents

A Special Note about how this book was created

Dear reader,

Thank you for buying your copy of *Ron Sukenick's Tips on Expanding your Business by Building Relationships.*

This book will teach you a bit about how to effectively use LinkedIn and how to network, both in the real and online worlds. You'll learn the reasons why networking is important and why you must effectively network to help your business expand.

This book was transcribed from a live interview.

That's why it reads as a conversation rather than a traditional "book" that talks "at" you.

Sincerely,

Richard Lowe Jr

Introduction
Interview

Ron's Sukenick's LinkedIn profile

Gold Star Referral Clubs

Richard Lowe (RL): I'd like to begin by talking about your work helping people with LinkedIn and being a published author.

Ron Sukenick (RS): A lit bit of my background; thank you, Richard, for asking, thank you, I grew up in New York, and ended up becoming part of the music business there. I moved over to Los Angeles and spent about 17 years in the music industry.

I was marketing for major recording studios in Los Angeles, and I had a unique ability to get out and connect with people, Always loved people, always loved being around people.

I moved into the world of networking back in the mid-70s, about 1975. That's when people were talking about this thing called networking, so I just jumped into it, liked it because it made sense to me.

I was in Vietnam in the '60's, and I ended up retiring from the United States Army Reserves.

I received a degree in marketing, so, you know I've been around marketing, advertising, and promotion, and I've been a VP of Sales and a VP of Marketing.

Many companies weren't doing very well, and I helped them do much better and achieved that through my ability to connect with people. Putting together channels of distribution. Getting better connected to people – it was something that interested me when I first started.

RL: How did you first start connecting? Were you always connecting with people or did you suddenly have a flash in your mind: I need to connect with people to make it?

RS: That's a good question. In fact, I should have gone back even further. I started my first business when I was five years old. I was living in the Bronx in New York.

For some reason, I wanted some money for candy and to go to the movies. Of course, in those days, it didn't take much, but it was a lot of money for a kid. I would ask my neighbors if I could take their garbage to the incinerator. Each person was paying me 10 cents a week, I ended up with 12 clients. 10 cents a week, 12 clients, I think that's about a buck twenty.

That was a lot of money for a kid because I could go to the movies for 50 cents which included plenty of money left over for candy.

I just loved people. I understood early on from the DISC model of human behavior that some people are moving at a faster pace than others; Some are people oriented; some are task oriented.

Then I've learned that there are those called introverts, and two-thirds of the population are your extroverts. You learn that in school, right, you learn things when you go to college. You start to understand people and it just starts to make sense. It just made sense.

I get energy from people. And I get involved on projects. I began to get involved in projects and to bring people together. I had this ability to bring people together over the years towards some common goals.

Then I got into the concept of networking; I began the expansion of the largest networking group, the most extensive networking referral system in the country. Today this group is known as BNI.

In those days, it was referred to as the network.

I began that expansion in 1988. We were known as the Network in California. I brought it to Indianapolis because that's where I was moving.

I've never been shy but you know everybody is such a unique blend of everybody else. I used my understanding of people as a way to adapt to people. I'm not here to change people, but I have enough strength and flexibility to adjust to other people. I can move at a slower pace, and I can be task oriented but what moves me is when I can go somewhere.

RL: Awesome.

RS: Where there are people I will go.

RL: You brought up several points, let me address a couple of them. One thing you've mentioned is you help people. I've interviewed several other networkers, and they all say the same thing. A vital part, perhaps the core of networking, is not what can you do for me, the essence of networking is how can I help you, and that, in turn, leads to down the road them helping – or reversing the flow. Would you say that's true? And why?

RS: It is. I guess that goes back to the Bible, like what they call a givers game philosophy. The fact is it's the very basic concept of reciprocity. You know the basis of most relationships is some form of exchange.

Richard, if I took you out, and bought you lunch one day, you might say, "hey, I'll buy lunch next time." That's just the way it is. And when you give to people, it triggers a chemical in the brain.

It creates some serotonin. Serotonin is what makes people feel good. So, the big payoff is when you take the networking concept - it's all about sharing ideas and information and resources.

You know, I'm a giver. And, unfortunately, a lot of the world is made up of people who are takers. So when the opportunity presents itself, I give. Giving is like an investment working for me over the years. Kind of like a savings account. If you invest in giving, there comes a time when you can withdraw the support you need from others.

You give them time and energy, you give them positive thoughts, I give them ideas, I connect dots. You know when you think about it, the power is clearly in the connection. A connection is not just between you and me – It's between you and I and something else.

I'm always looking for that something else. Whether we both love the Miami Dolphins or the Indianapolis Colts, or we both love just being an American, or we both love the Beatles, there's something. I always strive to go after the relationship and let me make another comment if I can, Richard.

RL: Of course

RS: In 2004 my first book was <u>Networking Your Way to Success</u>. The second book came out which was called <u>The Power Within the Connection</u> which was relationship focused. In fact, I built it around the philosophy of Net Being. B-E-I-N-G. Net Being.

That was a word that captures the essence of a relationship mindset. It is based on the premise that you have to be before you can do, you do to the extent of who you are, and who you are is based predominantly on how you think.

So the key to power, success and accomplishment is a method of thinking. But I've learned over the years that it's so much more fruitful when I go after relationships instead of sales.

Networking, in my opinion, is dead. I said it in 2004 when my 2nd book came out.

Consider this, it's awkward, it's hit and miss, it's situational, it always lacks support, and it's never about you.

The only thing that's left is to go after relationships. I mean if I ask 100 people in a room, "how many of you are here to sell something?" Everybody would raise their hand.

How about this question - "How many of you are here to buy something?" As you would imagine, most people don't raise their hand. So there's clearly a disconnect

Getting back to your original question, yeah, the gift is clearly in the giving and here's a quote, It's from Brian Tracy, a motivational speaker. He says, "Always give without remembering. Always receive without forgetting."

And when you give, you get people's attention, and when you get people's attention, it's a beginning process for making the connection.

RL: That's something I want to explore a little more. That connection. So it sounds like what you believe in is connecting people together, almost like the power broker, you could say. You're the person who sets up these two people to meet and in doing that you form the networks. Does that make sense?

RS: Well, yeah, a network is a system of elements. It's people that link together with common goals. So everybody has a shared purpose. The power for anybody that networks is to become purpose driven.

Here is a question for you - why do people go to a Chamber of Commerce meeting or Business After Hours or networking event? Well, they go there to better themselves.

So you take the concept of them wanting to better themselves and then what you do is help them in that process of bettering themselves.

That's the giver's main idea. They're there to better themselves. What they have to say is more important than what I have to say. I become the most interested person in the room, not the most interesting person. I'm going to become the most interested.

It gets people's attention. But the power today in the year 2016, is we have to continue to look for ways to become more useful and more resourceful to others. It's just the way it is.

I become more useful and resourceful. I have a need right now for a client of mine that needs somebody to ghostwrite a book. Well, what an unbelievable opportunity to know someone like you [a ghostwriter] that can get that done.

It's all about those eight magic words. Which is: I know someone that can get that done.

RL: I understand.

RS: That's where the money is. You know, you go to a store today, and you ask them if they have something. They say no and you say, well do you have any idea where I can get it. And more times than not they say "I don't know."

I believe today in business you have to come from knowing. We have to continue to look for ways to be useful and resourceful to others.

In my opinion, the desire for success hasn't changed. What's changing is how we get there. We're just better together.

There's not even a mystery about it. And I'll tell you another thing that's important in helping to get connected to others.

People are more vulnerable today than any other time in history. I mean that they're open. They're not defenseless, just open.

One of the results of being open is people are more approachable. And that's all built around a concept of social capital which is way down. So, it's an excellent time for people to connect in this county.

RL: What do you mean by social capital?

RS: Social capital is the glue that keeps communities together. You experience it in regards to associations and other organizations like Chambers and Churches.

Being that social capital is low, it's reflective in people not showing up at their meetings, and their membership is declining.

From a family standpoint, what about individuals who use to have people over to the house for dinner. You ever notice in the old days they used to do it all the time but today we don't because we live in a hurried society.

RL: A what society?

RS: A hurried society. Hurried. Isn't that a great word? Is it a good word?

RL: Never heard it before.

RS: Yeah. Just like bigly. I've never heard bigly either. But Donald Trump tends to use it. It's a real word, bigly.

RL: That's interesting.

RS: But, you know, SAT scores are higher when communities come together. There is less crime in communities when communities come together.

We've got people living in this country that don't even know who their neighbors are. That's how low social capital in this country has gotten. In fact, there was a book that was put out by a Harvard professor His name is Robert Putnam. He wrote a book called Bowling Alone.

He stated that a significant percent of our population bowls independent from leagues. In fact, he was predicting that over a short period, bowling leagues will become extinct because people are not coming together to bowl like they had in the past.

RL: Interesting.

RS: That was an interesting conversation, but that's what I mean when I say social capital. That's the glue that keeps families and communities together. So the key is to increase social capital.

What do you do? It's a very simple concept. Start having people over to your home, start hosting meetings, start getting involved in your church or whatever faith-based initiatives you go after. You get involved in projects, make a difference for veterans. That's what increases social capital.

RL: I see. Now, moving forward just a little bit; you've written books about LinkedIn, and you've talked about LinkedIn, and you promote LinkedIn. How does LinkedIn help your average business person or freelancer get ahead?

RS: Ok. And by the way, the LinkedIn book is <u>21 Days to Success with LinkedIn,</u> as I think you know, it's the second book in a series all put together through the eyes of a fictional character whose name happens to be Gnik Rowten, G-N-I-K-R-O-W-T-E-N. And if you spell his name backward, it spells networking.

It's kind of hidden meaning. In my first book which was <u>Networking Your Way to Success</u>, he was in the book, but he only said the eight magic words of networking, "I know somebody that can get it done."

In answer to your question about LinkedIn, it's pretty simple. LinkedIn is the largest professional database in the world.

If I look at LinkedIn's numbers, that's based on what they say, and it varies, it's growing, they've got 433 million people worldwide, about 128 million in our country here. They also have a geographic of 200 countries.

The number one activity on LinkedIn is searching for people. So either you're searching for people or people are searching for you. It's a pretty powerful engine when you think about it.

The way it's set up, it's predictable and reliable. Think about this - in the first quarter of 2016 you're looking at about 45 billion - that's with a "b" - page views.

And then the average time spent on LinkedIn worldwide is 17 minutes a month.

In my opinion, LinkedIn is underutilized and misunderstood.

LinkedIn started in May of 2003. I got on to LinkedIn in May of 2004. So, I was one of the first 200,000 people worldwide. Now why did I go onto LinkedIn? It seemed like the place to be. Right?

It's a free platform. There are also paid memberships that have premium features. There's a basic membership; you pay nothing, and you can get a lot of good stuff out of it but, you know for those that want to avoid making mistakes, here is what I suggest.

One is, they've got to understand why they are on LinkedIn. So, the "why" has got to be big enough. Whether you're a job seeker or maybe you just happen to be a freelancer looking for work. Maybe you want to do it for research.

But if you're looking for people it doesn't get much better. Once you know why you're on LinkedIn, you have to have a completed profile.

Most people that understand LinkedIn know that there are five different levels. Most people put only a little time and effort into it.

The highest level of completion is what they call All Star.

If your goal is to build an online digital reputation, you got to build your profile out. Of course, as you know, Richard, or at least I know that you know, you happen to be one of those writers that create profiles for people, right? So you know that.

You have to get it completed which gets you up to an all-star level.

After that, you then have to get it optimized which means when people search for you that they can find you. And then you've got to develop a connection strategy.

Most people don't even have that. I teach a lot, and I coach a lot, and I speak a lot on these topics.

A simple connection can be this: Connect with people you know, and connect with people you want to know.

I certainly want, from a connection standpoint, to utilize LinkedIn as a way to generate results. If I want business, I want to get business from it.

I found people who have found me on LinkedIn; socially it's proved out, digitally it's proved out, social proof because if somebody wants to hire me as a speaker or a trainer or a coach, I probably have about 50 different recommendations.

The great news is, it's not me saying how great I am, it's other people saying it. And I'm not talking about skills or endorsements. To me, it's an unbelievable tool to search out –

From a connection strategy standpoint, I don't connect with anybody unless they have a completed profile, they have a picture and at least a few recommendations.

You've got to have a connection strategy because here's what I find with some people; they have a tendency just to say, "oh I want a professional network", and they click "accept" or not. They may or may not even know the people, but it's like collecting business cards. What do people do with business cards? I think what they do is put a rubber band around them and throw them in their desk drawer.

RL: That's what I do with them.

RS: It doesn't work! So the key is, don't confuse activity for accomplishment. Everybody loves the joy of interaction. That's why we all do this.

I like to go to events and asking questions because it confirms the value of a relationship. In fact, it gives people joyful experiences of themselves. You know if I met you somewhere, and I start talking, and I notice that you have a business card that says The Writing King and the author of Real World Survival, Safe Computing, Inside Secrets for a Professional – all this kind of stuff I'd be blown away.

You're a blogger, an analyst, a ghost writer. In fact, I've got a lady friend of mine, before I forget, I'll introduce you to her. She has a company called Say It For You. She hires people. Virtually. Kind of like you're doing with Donna [from LinkedIn Makeover], if you're available. And she does a lot of blogging and a lot of ghostwriting.

She's a great writer; She's got a team of people all over the place. It's called Say It For You.

RL: Of course, I'm interested.

RS: If you make a note of that. Just look up Say It For You. Her name is Rhoda. Tell her you're a friend of mine. And she's an excellent friend of mine. She's known me about 25 years.

RL: What shouldn't you do with LinkedIn? You've talked about how you use LinkedIn but how do you use it wrong? Is there a way to use it incorrectly where it's not helping, even hurting you?

RS: Of course there is. Well, the biggest make mistake that I think some people make is they don't use it. That's a big mistake. You just don't accept connections – you know, you've got to engage with people. It's about communication.

Sometimes I ask people "what's the biggest investment you make when you build relationships with other people?"" They often don't understand that you have to invest time in people. So one mistake, I think, is just to click accept to any connection request.

If you want to accept it's fine but at least take a look at their profile. See they've [LinkedIn] got such a great system that when I look at your profile, Richard, you're going to know it because it says 'People that viewed your profile' right? You'll know that.

If you've got a premium level you can look at everybody that's looked at it. And if you're not on a premium membership you can see maybe 3-5 people at the most. But that's fine. At least you'll know that I looked at your profile.

Then what I would do is leave a comment. I say something like, "Hey Richard, thank you so much for taking a few moments to look at my profile. And thank you for the invite to get better connected. By the way, I just happened to notice that you happen to have written a book about "How to Operate a Freelance Writing Business and How to be a Ghostwriter" and I'd love to talk to you further about that. Maybe there's something we can do meaningful in 2016. Together.

Now if I did that, Richard, you'd be blown away I'd think. "Wow somebody actually responded back to you.

That's a mistake most people make. They just accept it, and that's it. They don't understand. In fact, with LinkedIn connections, I'm always interested in why people want to connect with me. I mean, I know I'm wonderful. I know people want to connect with me.

But what I do is I can talk to you without even accepting. There's a little box on the top right that I can click on and say, "Hey, Richard, thanks so much for the invite. I was just curious, was there anything in my profile that you found interesting? And was there any particular reason why you think we should connect?"

Right? I can do that. Because you see if I cancel you out, I can never get back to you again. You're out of my life forever according to how things are with LinkedIn. If I just x you out. If I don't know you, I don't know you. If you're spamming me, I'll put down that you're spamming me.

But, you know, just connecting is nothing so to me you've got to respond to people, you've got to thank people.

Another thing people don't do enough of is comment. People should be sharing content and sharing information. You know on LinkedIn you have as many followers as you have connections.

And on LinkedIn, you can also have more followers that you're not connected to because maybe they like what you've done in some of your publishing.

Using it incorrectly, in my opinion, is using it to attempt to sell people right off the bat. You know, they connect with you and the next thing you know they're trying to sell you stuff.

To me, I think it's important to go from high tech to high touch. Somebody living in Dallas Texas can connect with everybody in Dallas Texas. I can tell you how many people are on LinkedIn in Dallas, Texas; I can target my markets if I'm looking to sell, which is fine; but what I have to do is have some form of connection strategy.

What this means is I've got to go after the relationship which means I've got to understand you. I've got to at least share some content with you, get better connected to you. The more I know about you, the more likely it is we can help each other.

Then one day I say, "Hey Richard, I know we've been connected on LinkedIn since February, and I was just thinking we're both here in Dallas, are you familiar with the Starbucks over on 3rd Street?" You see, the suggestion now is to go from connecting on LinkedIn, to a face to face meeting at Starbucks.

How cool is that?

Again, going after the sell, just selling, is not the best strategy.

We live in a world where relationships increase the quality of life. I think everybody loves that. Nobody wants to be spammed. It's not a cocktail party like Facebook.

It's the definitive business professional network, and you don't have to spam people.

From a targeting standpoint, I can put together lists of up to 50 people and send direct messages to them. But you've got to share something which is meaningful to people. That's what interests people.

RL: You mentioned Facebook. How does LinkedIn fit into other social networks in a strategy? If somebody was putting together a networking strategy are there other social networks that they can use with LinkedIn?

RS: There are all kinds of social platforms. Whether it's Twitter, whether it's Tumblr, whether they're using YouTube or their using Google Plus. You could enrich it with media and add links to LinkedIn to connect it to other platforms, and there are things you can show from other platforms.

To me, Facebook is a cocktail party. Don't get me wrong. I like Facebook, and I'm always very interested in what people are doing. I can see what people are eating tonight or what they ate last night, how they feel about sports.

I can see who wants to make America great. I can see all the people who are hurting, just asking for prayers. On LinkedIn, I'm not going to see a lot of that stuff. It's more for business.

It's much more businesslike. To me, I think they all go together – look, in the world of networking or marketing, in general, you create a marketing mix. All advertising, marketing, and promotion pay. Some of it just pays more than others.

It's not just about putting up an ad and expecting results. I believe you engage with people. It's about engagement, it's about relationships, it's about facilitating communication. You know, you've got to be relevant. It's timely response.

I was coaching somebody the other day. They pay me money so I can coach them. They want to learn more about how to make the most from LinkedIn. She had - I've never seen this before Richard - 185 people wanting to connect with her. She's hasn't connected with anyone.

It makes no sense. I don't care what people think. They have privacy settings. You can hide from people. Do you want to hide from people? I had somebody a couple of weeks ago tell me that. They want to hide. They don't want people to know who they are. So, guess what? I told this person that he had no need to be on LinkedIn.

RS: So I tell him you're either LinkedIn or your LinkedOut. You're LinkedOut. You don't know why you're on LinkedIn; you're LinkedOut. You don't have a completed profile; if you're not LinkedIn, you're LinkedOut. You're not optimized; you're LinkedOut. In fact, if I were you I'd get the heck off of LinkedIn.

RL: And he paid you to say that.

RS: Yes. Sometimes people pay to tell them what they might already know, but just need someone to tell them what's best for them.

RL: It is funny. But one of my reasons for asking that is you only have so much time in a day. I already know that you believe you should Focus on LinkedIn if you're marketing your services or trying to network. What other networks are useful to use in your search for people of a like mind, so to speak?

RS: Business referral clubs are very popular and of course being active in associations and Chambers are always a good thing.

I'm currently involved with Gold Star Referral Clubs, and it's been the best decision I've made in years.

If you're in business, you need to join a business referral group.

RL: Let's think about other networks for a second. What kind of networks exist?

RS: Well, there's business networks like your Chamber of Commerce where you go for business. You've got your knowledge networks where you go to gain knowledge like the American Association of something or the National Association of something.

There are spiritual networks where you go to practice your faith.

There're service-related networks like the the Rotary, those Kiwanis people, you know, they're great people.

The Sertoma Clubs are a great organization. These people have been up and running since 1912, and they're there to serve humanity. The problem with them is social capital. Once again, declining memberships and nobody's got the time to help humanity anymore. So they're losing memberships all over the country.

There're some other veteran associations. They're networks too, right? These military assistance groups. And then there are social and political networks. So to me these social networks could be a singles club, it could be a fitness club, and that's a good way to network as well.

To build my body and my well-being, my strength and so forth. To me, it's all integrated. It's a marketing mix. I'm a big believer in LinkedIn because if I was in the recruiting business, I could find anybody anywhere in the world as long as their information happens to be in their profile.

If I'm looking for a ghostwriter within a 50-mile radius from whatever zip code I put in, or I want to find somebody in the country. You better have it in your profile for me to find it, right?

I'm sure if anybody knows that you do. To me I think they're all integrated, they all support one another. I think people like to watch videos. I just came back from doing a series of videos. Little 2-3 minute videos just talking about embracing the power of LinkedIn and whether you're LinkedIn or LinkedOut, That was the whole concept. Those were fast and furious, and I'll start to put them out in social media

RL: Interesting. You feel video is another way to network by producing videos to outflow information to other people?

RS: The bottom line for your success is you've got to be visible. You've got to be seen; you've got to be heard. That's why you're a writer. You're the Writing King, Richard. My god, I mean, pictures they can tell a thousand words, whatever that phrase is, right? So video is great. Anybody that does video they love the idea of talking about video. But it works beautifully. There's a lot of videos you can watch. Check out Ted Talks and see what that's all about.

RL: I love Ted Talks.

RS: I had a client today that was hurting, she's an introvert and she's afraid of asking for help - And I said, "I want you to go to YouTube right after this phone call. I want you to watch Steve Jobs and then put the word failure right next to it.

Steve Jobs, failure. You'll find the video. A minute and 47 seconds. And then we'll talk about what you just watched." And the bottom line, Steve Jobs talks about he's never gotten anything in his life without asking for help. And he noticed, in his lifetime, he'd never found anybody that wouldn't help him.

It goes back to a story with Hewlett-Packard when he was 12 years old. He wanted parts for a microprocessor or whatever he was doing at the time. A lot of people are afraid to ask for help.

RL: Why do you think that is?

Well because they don't want to impose on people. They believe everybody is busy, and they think there's nothing for them to offer in exchange – a lot of people in transition are that way. You know, they're underemployed or unemployed and for some reason, they think because they're out of work that there's nothing they bring to the table.

However, what they're bringing to the table is an opportunity for somebody to help them. And when we help people it makes us feel good. So people just don't want to impose.

That's why that whole concept of a who network, you know, a who network and I forget the guy's name but he started to talk about this thing called a who network. W-H-O. And the question is, who in your life are you neglecting.

The people that most people neglect are the people closest to them. Right? That's just the way it is. And the concept is that everybody that you need to get everything you need to get done, you already know. So it's possible that you don't need to meet anybody anymore.

Because everything you need to accomplish in life with the help of people you already have in you network.

Now, I must admit if you met me I've got about 6,000+ direct contacts on LinkedIn, and I can access about 30 million people. I meet people all the time. As a speaker and trainer, I'm in front of 30,000 people a year speaking.

In fact, I have a lady that I haven't seen in about 25 years. We reconnected. She runs a think tank, and she invited me to come in and talk about the power of LinkedIn. She invited 50 people to have lunch with me, It's all built around my topic and my work, so that's nice. Relationships never end, they just shift.

RL: You mentioned speaking. Is that something people should be doing more of? Speaking in public, speaking at the Rotary Club, speaking at their Toastmasters group?

RS: Of course

RL: Giving little speeches? Videos are impersonal; there's nobody there. There's nobody in front of you in a video, speaking you've got people in front of you, so it's a little bit different.

RS: It goes back again - the bottom line of all success is you've got to be visible. You've got to be seen; you've got to be heard. So, the concept of speaking is great if you enjoy speaking.

It all begins with having a passion for some topic. The heart fully develops before the brain. Your passion for the work you do resides in your heart. So if you're passionate about something – I mean, that's how I got my first book.

I was speaking about networking, my passion for being around people and this guy whose an acquisition editor for a company called, at the time, Kendal Hunt. A 50-million-dollar publishing company was jumping into the world of business books, and he thought this would make a great topic. And that's how my first book was born.

My second book was the Power Is In the Connection and then my third and fourth books were a result of speaking at an Association of Independent Information Professionals. And I met the acquisitions editor from Information Today publishing. He loved the message and said, "Wow I'd love to publish a book if you would write one."

So three of my four books were a result of my speaking, so it's just a significant part of the marketing mix. So, in answer to your question, if you enjoy speaking –

Look there's a ton of people out there that want to write books, they don't know how to write books. So there are five mistakes most people make when they're writing books. One of them just happens to be they can't write and maybe the biggest mistake they made was they didn't bring in a ghostwriter. Right?

RL: That makes sense.

RS: Yeah, so speaking is great. It works for me. I speak all the time, as often as I can. I'm a full-time professional speaker, and people pay me money. In fact, I raise my money every year now, Richard. Every year. As you get older you might as well charge more, right?

RL: Of course. I've found you're worth what you want to be worth. And you should ask…

RS: I've got a guy right now, one of my newest coaching clients. An interesting quick story. I met him 48 years ago. His cousin was a drummer in my band. I had a band. His cousin was a drummer in my band. His band was called the Vanilla Fudge. Their big hit was called "You Keep Me Hanging On" at the time.

RL: Yeah, I remember.

RS: Since then he moved on to play with Jeff Beck and Rod Stewart for years and Ozzy Osbourne. He's considered to one of the most revered rock and roll drummers of all time.

In the top 100, he's ranking 28 on the list but you know the bottom line is this: he wrote a book called Stick It!: My Life of Sex, Drums, and Rock 'n' Roll. He wants to get out from the drums. He's been drumming for 50 years.

I mean, that's a lot of effort. He's still drumming. But he wants something to happen with his book. He wants to get it promoted, marketed and he wants to speak. He wants to speak and he's got some great stories.

My job is to work with him, to get some of the comments some of the people are saying and some of the experiences he's had how do you translate it into a corporate environment? He' was asked by Jimmy Hendrix to come into Electric Lady Land to jam and in there was a girl by the name of Janis Joplin that was singing. In there was a guitar player by the name of Eric Clapton that was playing guitar.

They had the Winter Brothers. Both Jonny and Edgar Winter were in there. They were just jamming, and he was just this drummer playing drums.

The key to his success was surrounding himself with people who are being successful in his industry. That's what he did, and that's what kept him going all those years. So, the point I'm making, obviously, is he's wanting to utilize speaking because he can make money at speaking and it can help him with his book and his marketing all kinds of stuff.

RL: Interesting.

RS: His name, by the way, is Carmine Appice.

RL: Thank you. One of my favorite authors is Larry Winget, and he wrote a book, People are Idiots, and I Can Prove It and one of the things…

RS: Yeah he's good.

RL: One of the things he says is "if you want to be rich you need to hang out with rich people." Don't hang out with people who aren't rich. It sounds like you're saying sort of the same thing if you want to be whatever then you need to hang out with whatever kind of people.

RS: Look, there's a lot of victims in the world. I'm not interested in drama. I'm a creator of my experiences; I've got that. And I come from – everything I do in my life is a moment to moment choice. I've got that.

But I know I can't be in two different places at the same time, right? So I'm either happy or I'm not. I'm either doing what successful people do or I'm not. But that's what I chose to do.

I'm not interested in hanging out with people who are losing. I don't like being around takers. I don't like to be around people who don't have the integrity, and I stay away from these people.

I love to hang out with successful people. So, the answer to that is right. And I've always brought in people to work with that are smarter than me, much smarter. I've got a lady that's a business partner; that's a project manager for me, and she heads up an MBA program at a big university.

I've got another guy who ran a career center for a large pharmaceutical company for years to lead a team for me in regards to some of our training initiatives. These are people that are smarter than me.

I'm just good at bringing people together because I don't have a fear of making a mistake. I don't have a fear of talking to people.

I just have this ability to reach out and to connect and to come from – you know it's a place you come from. Networking is a place you come from; it's not a place you go to. It's not something you do sometimes and in some places. It's something we can do all the time and everywhere.

RL: Can you go into that in a little more detail?

RS: I could. It's like taking the moment and dancing with it. You know, that's what it's all about, right? To me, you come from what you're passionate about. I don't think of networking as a place or an event you go to. I think of it as a place you come from.

And if you took E.E. Cummings, who happens to be an American poet, he said: "you can teach anybody to think, believe and know but it's so difficult to teach people how to be."

For me, it's all about being. You know, I retired from the military. You had to be all you can be, right? That was a nice play on words. For me, I love the transformation, I love to challenge how I think, I love to challenge my assumptions and my beliefs.

I've heard this, we've all heard this – Charley Jones, I believe, was the guy who started this conversation – but you're who you are as a result of where you've been, people you've met, the books you've read, the tapes you listen to, and the experiences you have.

If I don't have any of those going on, I'm going to be the exact same person ten years from now as I am today. I want to enrich my life, and that's why I love this concept of networking. That's what's so great about networking.

I get to access people; I get to meet more and more people. It's all about the joy of interaction; it's fun.

RL: Ah. Alright, do you have any training or reading that you'd recommend to our listeners or readers in this case?

RS: When you say training or readings, there are so many suggestions I would make –

From a training standpoint, look at Dale Carnegie training to get better at working with people.

I like personality insights out of Atlanta to become DISC Trained – DISC is a model of human behavior.

From reading, of course, any of my books –The E-Myth by Michael Gerber and too many others to mention.

I want to say from a business standpoint the organization that I've been part of since 2009 they're called Gold Star Referral Clubs; they meet weekly to build relationships and refer business to one another. You know, when you talk about the networks like you said, there are these business networks and there are these things called referral groups.

If you break it down, you've got strong and casual contact groups. The casual ones are the Chamber groups; everybody is just meeting everybody. And then you've got the referral groups that meet weekly to build relationships and refer business. So Goldstarreferralclubs.com is what's exploding right now. I think they've got 100 clubs in 15 states.

The distinction between them and other referral clubs is just they've got a shorter meeting with fewer rules, more fun and people can pay monthly. But referral clubs are big. That's what I would suggest that's what they do. Did that answer your question?

RL: Yes. Are there any – let's look at each piece. You recommend joining a local networking group like a referral club or a....

RS: Oh yeah, I mean, if you're looking for referral business because I think we all meet people best through recommendations, so become a member of the chamber is good because that promotes an economic welfare in a community.

Also, be targeted into a knowledge network so if I'm an HR consultant, I would think I would join SHRP Society for Human Resource Professionals, right? I mean that's what I would do.

If I'm a trainer or a facilitator I want to join an Association of Training and Development, AISTD.

You want to get into knowledge networks because you want to get smack into your industry, you want to be with your peers. You want to get into a referral group if you're looking for business referrals and then you want to promote economic welfare in a community.

You've got to include it as part of your marketing strategy, so it's just got to be part of your planning. That's what I would recommend to people. And then I would recommend that they have an online presence and keep it updated and give updates and publish stuff and be on LinkedIn. And then, of course...

RL: And…

RS: Go ahead.

RL: And, of course, they should read your books.

RS: They could. They could go to my website www.ronsukenick.com and figure out who I am and what I'm about but for anyone reading this interview it would be perfect for them to go, "Wow, what an interesting person. Let's invite him to come out and speak."

I go anywhere in the world. I was just on the phone with a planner in Hawaii that wants me to go to Guam. I've been to Guam 3 times. I go to Guam it's only 17 hours by plane.

RL: I suppose you'd recommend joining Toastmasters to learn how to speak or taking training on LinkedIn, all those kinds of things.

RS: Yeah, Toastmasters a great organization. – I've been to Toastmasters meetings, but I bypassed Toastmasters and went directly to the National Speakers Association.

RL: Of course.

RS: Because I wanted to model myself after people who are doing it, that are making money at it. But I will say that Toastmasters is clearly a great organization. And for anybody that – if they want to get into the world of speaking, and they're kind of shy with their presentations they're going to count all the times that you go "uh, uh, uh, uh." They're going to come up with these words of the day. It's unbelievable; it's just a great organization.

RL: Yeah, I'm a member of it. I've got to give a speech next week.

RS: Yeah, yeah and you'll probably do great. And you'll get critique. And it's great, what a great life. Get critique.

RL: The give excellent critiques. It's a positive, uplifting critique from a group of friends. It's wonderful.

RS: Yeah.

RL: Alright, well, I think we're getting close to being out of time. Is there anything else you'd like to add in closing?

RS: No, I think we've covered a lot of stuff. Right now, I'm excited about the power of LinkedIn, so I'm just talking a lot about it. I'm helping people a lot. And, you know, for yourself, Richard, you might look at AIIP; that's a pretty cool group. You might find it – Association of Independent Information Professionals. But, no, I just think that if there were any closing comments, you know you just become a giver. You look for more ways to become resourceful and useful to people. And I find that the more people I meet, the more opportunities I have to help others.

RL: Interesting.

RS: That's it. I mean it's that simple. No mystery behind any of it.

RL: Very interesting. Ok, well, thank you for the interview.

RS: You are very welcome. Thank you for the opportunity to share my insights into the networking process.

Before you go

If you scroll to the last page in this eBook, you will have the opportunity to leave feedback and share the book with Before You Go. I'd be grateful if you turned to the last page and shared the book.

Also, if you have time, please leave a review on Amazon. Positive reviews are incredibly useful. If you didn't like the book, please email me at rich@thewritingking.com and I'd be happy to get your input.

About the Author

About the Author

https://www.linkedin.com/in/richardlowejr
Feel free to send a connection request

Follow me on Twitter: @richardlowejr

Richard Lowe has leveraged more than 35 years of experience as a Senior Computer Manager and Designer at four companies into that of a bestselling author, blogger, ghostwriter, and public speaker. He has written hundreds of articles for blogs and ghostwritten more than a dozen books and has published manuscripts about computers, the Internet, surviving disasters, management, and human rights. He is currently working on a ten-volume science fiction series – the Peacekeeper Series – to be published at the rate of three volumes per year, beginning in 2016.

Richard started in the field of Information Technology, first as the Vice President of Consulting at Software Techniques, Inc. Because he craved action, after six years he moved on to work for two companies at the same time: he was the Vice President of Consulting at Beck Computer Systems and the Senior Designer at BIF Accutel. In January 1994, Richard found a home at Trader Joe's as the Director of Technical Services and Computer Operations. He remained with that incredible company for almost 20 years before taking an early retirement to begin a new life as a professional writer. He is currently the CEO of The Writing King, a company that provides all forms of writing services, the owner of The EBay King, and a Senior Branding Expert for LinkedIn Makeover. You can find a current list of all books on his Author Page and take a look at his exclusive line of coloring books at The Coloring King.

Richard has a quirky sense of humor and has found that life is full of joy and wonder. As he puts it, "This little ball of rock, mud, and water we call Earth is an incredible place, with many secrets to discover. Beings fill our corner of the universe, and some are happy, and others are sad, but each has their unique story to tell."

His philosophy is to take life with a light heart, and he approaches each day as a new source of happiness. Evil is ignored, discarded, or defeated; good is helped, enriched, and fulfilled. One of his primary interests is to educate people about their human rights and assist them to learn how to be happy in life.

Richard spent many happy days hiking in national parks, crawling over boulders, and peering at Indian pictographs. He toured the

Channel Islands off Santa Barbara and stared in fascination at wasps building their homes in Anza-Borrego. One of his joys is photography, and he has photographed more than 1,200 belly dancing events, as well as dozens of Renaissance fairs all over the country.

Because writing is his passion, Richard remains incredibly creative and prolific; each day he writes between 5,000 and 10,000 words, diligently using language to bring life to the world so that others may learn and be entertained.

Richard is the CEO of The Writing King, which specializes in fulfilling any writing need. You can find out more at https://www.thewritingking.com/, and emails are welcome at rich@thewritingking.com

Books by Richard G Lowe Jr.

Business Professional Series

On the Professional Code of Ethics and Business Conduct in the Workplace – Professional Ethics: 100 Tips to Improve Your Professional Life - have you ever wondered what it takes to be successful in the professional world? This book gives you some tips that will improve your job and your career.

Help! My Boss is Whacko! - How to Deal with a Hostile Work Environment - sometimes the problem is the boss. There are all kinds of managers, some competent, some incompetent, and others just plain whacked. This book will help you understand and handle those different types of managers.

Help! I've Lost My Job: Tips on What to do When You're Unexpectedly Unemployed – suddenly having to leave your job can be a harsh and emotional time in your life. Learn some of the things that you need to consider and handle if this happens to you.

Help! My Job Sucks Insider Tips on Making Your Job More Satisfying and Improving Your Career – sometimes conditions conspire to make the regular trek to a job feel like a trip through Dante's Inferno. Sometimes, these are out of our control, such as a malicious manager or incompetent colleague. On the other hand, we can take control of our lives and workplace and improve our situation. Get this book to learn what you can do when your job sucks.

How to Manage a Consulting Project: Make money, get your project done on time, and get referred again and again – I found that being a consultant is a great way to earn a living. Managing a consulting project can be a challenge. This book contains some tips to help you so you can deliver a better product or service to your customers.

How to be a Good Manager and Supervisor, and How to Delegate – Lessons Learned from the Trenches: Insider Secrets for Managers and Supervisors – I've been a manager for over thirty years I learned many things about how to get the job done and deliver quality service. The information in this book will help you manage your projects to a high level of quality.

Focus on LinkedIn – Learn how to create a LinkedIn profile and to network effectively using the #1 business social media site.

Home Computer Security Series

Safe Computing is Like Safe Sex: You have to practice it to avoid infection – Security expert and Computer Executive, Richard Lowe, presents the simple steps you can take to protect your computer, photos and information from evil doers and viruses. Using easy-to-understand examples and simple explanations, Lowe explains why hackers want your system, what they do with your information, and what you can do to keep them at bay. Lowe answers the question: how to you keep yourself say in the wild west of the internet.

Disaster Preparation and Survival Series

Real World Survival Tips and Survival Guide: Preparing for and Surviving Disasters with Survival Skills – CERT (Civilian Emergency Response Team) trained and Disaster Recovery Specialist, Richard Lowe, lays out how to make you, your family, and your friends ready for any disaster, large or small. Based upon specialized training, interviews with experts and personal experience, Lowe answers the big question: what is the secret to improving the odds of survival even after a big disaster?

Creating a Bug Out Bag to Save Your Life: What you need to pack for emergency evacuations - When you are ordered to evacuate—or leave of your free will—you probably won't have a lot of time to gather your belongings and the things you'll need. You may have just a few minutes to get out of your home. The best preparation for evacuation is to create what is called a bug out bag. These are also known as go-bags, as in, "grab it and go!"

Professional Freelance Writer Series

How to Operate a Freelance Writing Business, and How to be a Ghostwriter – Proven Tips and Tricks Every Author Needs to Know about Freelance Writing: Insider Secrets from a Professional Ghostwriter – This book explains how to be a ghostwriter, and gives tips on everything from finding customers to creating a statement of work to delivering your final product.

How to Write a Blog That Sells and How to Make Money From Blogging: Insider Secrets from a Professional Blogger: Proven Tips and Tricks Every Blogger Needs to Know to Make Money – There is an art to writing an article that prompts the reader to make a decision to do something. That's the narrow focus of this book. You will learn how to create an article that gets a reader interested, entices them, informs them, and causes them to make a decision when they reach the end.

Other Books by Richard Lowe Jr

How to Be Friends with Women: How to Surround Yourself with Beautiful Women without Being Sleazy – I am a photographer and frequently find myself surrounded by some of the most beautiful women in the world. This book explains how men can attract women and keep them as friends, which can often lead to real, fulfilling relationships.

How to Throw Parties like a Professional: Tips to Help You Succeed with Putting on a Party Event – Many of us have put on parties, and I know it can be a daunting and confusing experience. In this book, I share what I learned from hosting small house parties to shows and events.

Additional Resources

Is your career important to you? Find out how to move your career in any direction you desire, improve your long-term livelihood, and be prepared for any eventuality. Visit the page below to sign up to receive valuable tips via email, and to get a free eBook about how to optimize your LinkedIn profile.

http://list.thewritingking.com/

I've written and published many books on a variety of subjects. They are all listed on the following page.

https://www.thewritingking.com/books/

On that site, I also publish articles about business, writing, and other subjects. You can visit by clicking the following link:

https://www.thewritingking.com

To find out more about me or my photography, you can visit these sites:

Personal website: https://www.richardlowe.com
Photography: http://www.richardlowejr.com
LinkedIn Profile: https://www.linkedin.com/in/richardlowejr
Twitter: https://twitter.com/richardlowejr

If you have any comments about this book, feel free to email me at rich@thewritingking.com

Premium Writing Services

Do you have a story that needs to be told? Have you been trying to write a book for ages but never can seem to find the time to get it done? Do you want to brand your business, but don't know how to get started?

The Writing King has the answer. We can help you with any of your writing needs.

Ghostwriting. We can write your book, which entails interviewing you to get your story, writing the book and then working with you to revise it until complete. To discuss your book, contact The Writing King today.

Website Copy. Many businesses include the text on their sites as an afterthought, and that can result in lost sales and leads. Hire The Writing King to review your site and recommend changes to the text which will help communicate your message and improve your sales.

Blogging. Build engagement with your customers by hiring us to write a weekly or semi-weekly article for your blog, LinkedIn or other social media. Contact The Writing King today to discuss your blogging needs.

LinkedIn. LinkedIn is of the most important vehicles for finding new business, and a professionally written profile works to pulling in those leads. Write or update your profile today.

Technical Writing. We have broad experience in the computer, warehousing and retail industries, and have written hundreds of technical documents. Contact The Writing King today to find out how we can help you with your technical writing project.

The Writing King has the skills and knowledge to help you with any of your writing needs. Call us today to discuss how we can help you.

www.ingramcontent.com/pod-product-compliance
Lightning Source LLC
Chambersburg PA
CBHW071520210326

41597CB00018B/2824